This book is dedicated to my younger self. The little girl with dreams, big brown eyes, and a people pleasing streak a mile wide. You grew up and you made it, little one. I am so fiercely proud of the woman you have become, and all that you have lived through. You, my little girl, are my hero.

To the people who loved me, before I ever really knew how to love myself, thank you. You are loved and appreciated beyond measure.

D1527343

It's Going to be Great! It's Fine, I'm Fine
A Survive and Thrive Guide
Lisa Scott, LPC

Introduction

If you have asked yourself time and time again, what the hell am I doing

with my life then you are definitely not alone. Everyday women struggle

to figure things out and somedays just end up with even more questions

about who they are, where they are going, if they will ever find love, if

they will ever feel worthy, and when things will stop being such a

struggle.

The pain and confusion of the pressures and struggles for most can

feel paralyzing some days. Some days it actually feels like you have

thrown gas on the dumpster fire you have labeled as your life, and you

didn't even mean to. Right now, you may be thinking that things will

never get better and you're too far down in the dumps to get things on

track, but let me tell you, it does get better. You don't just have to survive,

you can actually find empowerment and joy in learning how to thrive.

Thriving can look like, knowing exactly who you are and feeling a sense of pride. It can look like setting boundaries with friends and co workers that don't result in a seven day anxiety attack over the fact you may have offended someone. Thriving feels good and allows you to roll with the ups and downs that life has a tendency to throw your way when you didn't want it or least expect it. Thriving comes in all shapes and sizes and gets to look how you define it to be. It is about claiming your worth, your value, and your place on this planet.

I am challenging you to keep an open mind and heart, and follow me as I teach you the tools to walk out of the flames of your past like wonder woman on a mission.

Life has a way of never really working out the way that we thought it would, and when that happens we have an opportunity to learn about ourselves and others. When we are brave enough to look in the mirror and be proud of who we see, the world starts to look a lot different. It begins to look like a place of opportunity and growth versus a wasteland of missed opportunity and longing to be like someone else. Thinking things like, if only I had their job, their clothes, their waist size, or their family I could thrive, too. I'm here to tell you with great confidence, that longing for what you think someone else is thriving with, is missing an opportunity to thrive in your own life. Waiting for things you think will make you happy, leaves you in a constant state of setting yourself up to never be enough in your own mind.

It's hard to pick just one thing that inspired me to write this book. I am a daughter, a girlfriend, a step mom, and a therapist, to name a few. I think I have always known that I had a book in my heart but could never really pinpoint where that energy should go. Self worth, troubled childhoods, and relationship struggles are the top three reasons I see many of my clients in private practice. The emotional pain and the road to growth for these young women has really touched my heart and often times motivated me to take the extra client, work the extra day and to always continue to learn about growth, empowerment and change.

Before I became a therapist and even in the beginning of my career, I too struggled through my twenties and thirties, and know all too well the kind of shame and pain accompany life's rocky journey, and the pressures woman face to get the job, have the kids, appear put together, and work harder than most to prove her place in this world. I made choices that weren't becoming of me, I struggled with being proud of who I was consistently, and suffered too often in silence for fear of telling anyone my vulnerabilities that may appear to paint me as weak. I chased people who didn't deserve my emotional investment, and structured a life around a subconscious story about needing to be the best to prove my worth and value on this planet and in peoples' lives.

It wasn't until I was doing some inner child work with a client that I started to think about my own inner child and started to see the cracks in the work that I thought I had done to make peace with my father's roll or lack there of in my child hood. I brought this up to a colleague later that day after the session. I explained that while I really thought I had worked through my childhood and self worth concerns after my marriage ended, I was so moved by the client I was working with today, that I am starting to think there is more work to do. My colleague tilted his head and gave me half a smile, and said, "Lisa, you are the best therapist and probably one of the strongest people I know, but to hear you say you might have some more work to do, is music to my ears."

I can remember thinking, uhhhhh what the hell does that mean? Does everyone see I still have some residual wounds from the past? He smiled again, and said, "I don't want you to take this the wrong way, but look at the guys you date. They don't align or measure up to the kind of woman you are. You know better than most, that to change a pattern you have to look back on why you engage it in the first place."

He was right. I was in my early thirties at this point and when I got really honest with myself, he was absolutely right. I was still holding on to this perceived sense of worth, one that was dependent on how strong I was, how funny I was, and what I could do for other people. In other words, I chased losers who didn't want to be caught, and had a touchy relationship with my own self worth.

That was the start of the rest of my growth and of connecting to an intensely loving connection to my self worth. I spent the next several months looking honestly at my life, my choices, and where I wanted to be. I did this work, in an effort to understand myself not shame myself. I put the work in, I cried the tears and took accountability. If I hand't had that conversation I don't think it would have pushed me to finish my work, and I wouldn't be sitting here today, writing to you as a woman who feels whole, and internally calm even during some of the biggest stressors that are thrown my way.

I want you to come along on a journey with me as I teach you everything I have learned and so much more. I was always taught that therapists shouldn't share their story in an effort to be objective and keep the client as a priority, and while I mostly agree with this while in a session with a client, I am a big fan of the right time and right place, and this book is the right time and the right place. Life is personal. Life is beautiful, and so is your story. Get excited about what's to come! Let's do this!

How to Read This Book

Each chapter of this book is meant to provide explanations, but also get you thinking about why you're currently navigating the world like you are, and how you could better that navigation. As you read this book, I want you to get very comfortable asking yourself, WHY. Why did I do that, why did I repeat that? Asking yourself why is a way to not only better connect to and get to know yourself, but it is an opportunity to create self compassion and connect to your innate worth. In each chapter I will provide tools and exercises for you to work through. If you take your time, and open your heart to trying some new things and letting some old things go, then you can plan to finish this book feeling worthy, feeling valued,

and feeling empowered about where you'll go next. This book is not

meant to replace therapy with a counselor in a 1:1 setting, it's meant to

provide you some things to think about and become self aware. Being self

aware allows you the space to get curious about yourself and the world

around you, and it's that curiosity that will help you start to make changes.

Chapter 1

Lost Sheep to Shepard, Come in Shepard

Have you ever seen a field of sheep out in the middle of nowhere? They stick together, move in a herd and look cute and fluffy while doing it. What we don't see from the outside is that they long for someone to lead them, a Shepard, that tells them where to go and provides them with things like food and shelter. Right now, I would venture to guess that you are feeling a lot like those sheep. You might look cute and fluffy from the outside, but inside you long to find someone to show you the way, to take care of you, and give you some purpose. I want you to get comfortable with the idea, that the person who is going to lead you and provide for you, is none other than yourself.

Finding your place in this world, means connecting to and knowing your worth and what makes you, you. Until you can get comfortable with the idea that you are going to lead yourself and love it, you will stay lost in a herd just waiting for someone to save you. Plot twist, *you* get to save yourself!

When you navigate the world disconnected from your worth, you navigate lost and going with the herd, waiting to be led. Let me be clear, self worth isn't something you have or you don't have, it is something you are born with. All of us! You were born innately worthy, which is great news, because contrary to what you may have picked up in childhood, you don't have to earn it or find it, it's already yours to reach up claim. Innate means, inborn or natural, and worth means value. Put together those two words work together to tell you that you were born with natural value.

The problem with the notion that self worth is something you earn, means you place it in other people's hands. You place your worth in this world, in somebody's else's hands, and that is not sustainable for an empowered authentic life. Just as bad as placing your worth is other's hands is also placing it based on things you own, jobs you have, your outward appearance etc. I think, a lot of people place their innate worth in outside things and people and don't even realize it, until they get to a point in their life, where they say this isn't working and I don't know how to feel better. This first place I always start to look at and examine with my clients, is how connected they are their innate worth.

A lot of people tell me, I know I'm worthy and deserve good people and good things, this isn't a self worth problem. That is always my cue to ask them how they feel their choices in life align with their worth. For example, are they able to sit and be present with themselves in a space of compassion and love or is their internal dialogue a negative harsh one? Can you honestly tell me that you treat yourself as well as you treat others around you? It is most always right then and there that most people have this realization, that they aren't very nice to themselves. They are hard on themselves and shame themselves for mistakes, missed milestones, and various events from the past. There is nothing wrong with you for doing this, it just means that there is an opportunity to reset and reconnect to your innate worth. There is an opportunity to treat yourself the way you long to be treated in relationships.

Most people I encounter tell me they want to be be in a safe, loving, respectful, connected, healthy, fun relationship with someone else. Clients tell me that they want to be with someone who is emotionally mature and can have difficult conversations in order to grow together and stay connected. It seems easier for most to know how they want to feel and how they want to be treated in a relationship, but when it comes to cultivating that relationship with ourselves it seems to fall apart a bit. Developing this kind of relationship with yourself takes time, accountability, effort, and energy.

Often times, it's difficult to look back and see where you disconnected from your worth. I say disconnected, because that's what happened. Along the way, people and experiences caused you to subconsciously and sometimes consciously question your worth, which started the disconnection. Before you knew it, you were so far off track from your worth that the decisions you were making and continue to, are for other people in an effort to feel safe and to feel valid and worthy. The survival of your worth, almost overnight, is dependent on receiving something, whether that be validation from others or purchasing a fancy car, having a job with social status etc. The trouble here, is that while that validation may feel good in the moment, it is fleeting, because once that high wears off, you are left empty again, which triggers you to run back outside on a mission of chasing that feeling of being valid and worthy.

It took me well into my thirties to grasp this concept and get reconnected, so I hope to save some of you some time here. Before you start thinking it's too late and too much life has been lived or damage done, I need you to know that right now is right on time, and it's never too late to take your power back and bring the relationship with your worth and value inside, where it belongs and where you are in control.

It wasn't until I was in my mid thirties that I started to understand the motivation for a lot of my choices. I was the consummate people pleaser. For a while I justified it by telling myself that I liked to do things for others and that made me feel good. It wasn't until I realized I needed their approval to feel worthy that I started to take a deeper look and realized, that I still got to be a kind hearted person who did for others but never at the expense of my own mental health and certainly never again to feel like I have earned my place or to feel worthy. Constantly doing things for others or out of fear of someone's reaction or judgment to my actions, actually put me in a marriage that wasn't healthy and got me so off course and disconnected to my worth, that is just about cost me everything.

In high school, before going out my mom used to tell me that sometimes people respect you more for what you don't do than what you choose to do. At the time I had a vague idea of what she was trying to convey, and it took me a long time to understand what mattered most is that I respected myself.

I grew up in a midwestern home, with divorced parents. I was the younger of two girls and then the second oldest when my mom married my step dad when I was about ten years old. My biological dad was in and out of our lives, and when he was around was scary. He easily angered, and was physically abusive to my mother. He was emotionally and verbally abusive to everyone that I knew around us, and could spark a feeling of terror in me as a child that thankfully I haven't had replicated again in my life today. As a five year old, I didn't have the experience or worldview of an adult to know that how he behaved and treated me wasn't ok. I knew it scared me, and I knew things like, if I fell and got hurt I was in big trouble and I better be afraid. I knew that if I made a mistake or couldn't find something he asked me to get for him, I was in trouble and the feeling of terror would return. Looking back I think I almost terrorized myself more anticipating all of the ways I would get in trouble, than the actual event of being yelled at and shamed.

As a five year old, my brain was on the constant look out to keep me safe, and with such a limited world view, it did what it knew how to do at five years old, and told me, if you can lighten the mood and make him laugh the yelling will stop. If you can be perfect and steal the show, he will be proud. If you can race down the hallway and draw a picture of a happy family while he is hitting mom then maybe he will stop. If you sit in the front yard and wait for him to pick you up when he said he would, then surely he will come for you, and if he doesn't, you're absolutely sure he wanted to but just couldn't make it.

When we are children we learn coping skills and strategies that don't always serve us in adulthood, because our behavior and emotions are meshed together. I learned if I could be the shining star and do things for people, solve problems faster, excel in sports, stay perfect or project an image of perfection then I would feel safe and worthy. The problem with this line of thinking, is that it didn't serve me in adulthood and only left me feeling lonely, and more often than not less than. In a sense I still had a five year old in my heart trying to manage my adult life, and that wasn't working. It worked pretty well to calm the monster down and feel accepted and wanted as a kid, but it wasn't it working now.

What's even worse though, is that no matter how much I tried to be the best or to wow my peers or dates, when it didn't work I was left with the feeling of shame and rejection. I was left feeling like there was something wrong with me. The feeling of shame is a heavy one, and when left alone with too much of it, the disconnect from your worth goes from a disconnect all the way to a canyon miles deep that you have no idea how to climb out of.

And so it went, I found very few people in my adult life that I felt I could really be myself around. Most of that being my fault, because I really had only a vague idea of who I was under all of the pleasing and working tirelessly to be seen as enough. I was good at friendship, and terrible at romantic relationships. I always seemed to wind up with the "bad boy" or people that were emotionally unavailable. Seeking people out who are emotionally unavailable is a sign that I was emotionally unavailable to myself and what I was worthy of. At the time I thought the problem was me not being enough for them, and if I could show them how great I was they would stay, but they rarely did. I knew I didn't want to end up with a guy like my dad. I wouldn't tolerate physical abuse or yelling, but what I didn't know yet, is that my emotional brain thought it knew how to excel in situations where people were inconsistent and unavailable, so every time I would find someone that would show some interest then disappear my emotional memory kicked in subconsciously and said, "hey, we know just what to do here!" While I know now, that terrible taste in men actually means terrible taste in myself, it took me quite a few exhausting chases to figure it out. I stopped asking why does this keep happening to me, and started asking myself why I allowed it?

In life, connecting to your worth, means choosing yourself everyday. It means behaving in a way that is becoming of you, that takes care of you, and that doesn't shame yourself. It looks like being able to see someone else's behavior as a reflection of them, and not an indiction of your worth. At first, this new found ability to choose and love yourself may feel like arrogance, only because you aren't used to it. It can feel uncomfortable and selfish to put yourself first and have confidence in the person you are, but that is temporary and you will start to see that you can put yourself first, and still continue to be a kind thoughtful individual. You can choose yourself first and then decide from a place of empowerment if you want to invite someone else in because you want to, not because you feel like you have to.

In the relationships I struggled with, even though the physical behavior wasn't the same as with my dad, the emotional feeling was, and it's those patterns that we tend to repeat over and over until we realize why we do it and how to stop it. What it took for me, was to think back to one of the first times as a child I thought pleasing and being perfect would fix things and get my dad to pick me. When I could pin point that, I could pinpoint where I started to disconnect from my innate worth and put conditions on my worth. I sat with that image and pictured my big innocent brown eyes. I connected to the emotion I must have been feeling as an innocent child, not knowing any better and just wanting to be enough for him, and I cried. I wrote my five year old self a letter and told her she was perfect the way she was and didn't need to prove herself to anyone. I told her that she was worthy of more than what she was given, and I gave her permission to be a child and to take the pressure off of being perfect or a fixer. In a sense, I became the adult I needed as a child.

I have that letter to this day, and even now when there are times I am triggered to fix something for someone or go above and beyond to prove my place, I think about that letter and that little girl, and I whisper, "You're ok, I am proud of you, You are enough." In the beginning I whispered that little phrase a million times a day to redirect myself and slow down. I whispered that to train myself to connect to the worth I was born with and to allow myself to be me and to be enough. I learned that my worth was not conditional, and putting it in other people's hands wasn't taking care of it, but rather giving my power and my story away to someone who couldn't take care of it. I was the one who needed to reach up and grab it, and start making choices that honored it.

In my private practice, I support a lot of people who have no idea that they were born worthy, and no idea that they were even really that disconnected from it. It's only when we start to establish patterns they are repeating that they start to see they aren't choosing themselves, but rather trying to prove themselves or hide, for fear of not being enough or not being chosen. In order to start to value yourself you have to know who you are. While I am sure on the surface, many of us think we know who we are, I would challenge you to think about that. I want to challenge you to quiet the outside noise of your family, friends, co worker, partners, and most of society and just sit with yourself in a quiet place for a few minutes. Soften your body and let the tension go, take a deep breath and remind yourself you were born worthy. Then I want you to start to write down, what makes you, YOU. Make a list of values you believe in and can adhere to, make a list of the qualities in which you are proud of and then keep that list close. This list is the new roadmap that will help you to make choices that honor you and your worth. The thing here, is that you don't have to be perfect, just human.

The bottom line is that if you are struggling with self worth, then it's safe to say it's something life has taught you that you have to find outside of yourself. If your self worth and self identity are reliant on outside things then you will always be chasing the next thing to feel worthy. The next job, the next relationship, the next fashion trend, the next whatever, and when that feeling fades or you aren't able to obtain the next thing, you're left with feeling less than and shameful, and your life is made up of a chronic chase for worth and value in this world.

I see a lot of people who think that to fill the emptiness this cycle creates they just work harder or try more to be liked, however I would challenge you to think about the return on investment with spending your energy like this. When you spend your life chasing outside things, the result will be feelings of emptiness, loneliness, and shame. Give yourself the opportunity, today, to start asking Who am I? Where did I learn this? What are my values? Why do I do this?. This line of questioning will start to lead you down a road of self discovery and self connection and growth. Challenge yourself today to start to shift your energy from outside factors and turn inward. Soften your approach to yourself as you learn and get curious about yourself and where the disconnect from your worth happened.

The disconnect is going to be a different sum of experiences for everyone. Some may look back and see that the disconnect started in childhood and continued into adulthood, while others may look back and see that the disconnect started to happen later in life after a difficult experience or relationship. Think about this process like pulling weeds out of a garden. You can pull the top off but the root is still there and therefore that won't get rid of the weed. It might for a little while, but until you can get down to the root or the why, of why the weed grew in the first place it will continue to come back and destroy the beauty around it. You have an opportunity here to go deeper than you have before and get accountable for the patterns you repeat and the choices you make that are or aren't becoming of your worth.

W - Wake up ready to love and connect with yourself

O - Open you heart to yourself, take a breath and soften your body

R - Review your internal dialogue and make sure it's supportive and loving

T - Take time each day to be proud of yourself

H - Hype yourself up! Look in the mirror and tell yourself things like " I LOVE YOU, I'M PROUD OF YOU, YOU ARE WORTHY, YOU ARE OK, YOU ARE VALUABLE."

Assignment #1

Grab a journal and pen or pencil and get ready to do some old fashioned

hand writing. I'd encourage you to purchase a journal that feels like it's

special. Maybe that's a leather bound journal or one with an inspirational

quote on it or even a regular notebook in your favorite color, just make

sure it's something you dedicate for you and your story. Start to explore

the questions raised in this chapter about your past and start directing your

energy inward. I want you to remember and understand that as children

our behavior and feelings are meshed. How our behavior was managed

created the foundation for how you relate to yourself and your emotions.

Start to think about where and how you may have gone off track with

valuing yourself and how has that spilled over into the patterns you repeat in your adult life. This isn't an exercise to blame your parents, this is an exercise in meeting yourself and your story with self compassion and reconnecting and reclaiming your worth and identity.

There are no right or wrong answers here. Just start writing down and brainstorming patterns that aren't working for you, but you tend to see yourself making over and over. Then ask yourself, why? What need am I trying to meet, what are my fears, what is my payoff and how can I start to recognize these patterns as I find myself in them, and start to hold myself accountable to making different choices. How can I make choices rooted in self worth and that are becoming of my value and who I am.

Chapter 2

Shame always equates to a negative return on investment.

A lot of people I come across in private practice use shame as a motivator of sorts. They feel like if they are hard on themselves it must mean they are disciplined. I couldn't disagree more, and know both personally and professionally the cost of shame. It erodes your connection to your innate worth, it sets you up to fail almost constantly, and it robs you of a place of acceptance and unconditional love for yourself as you navigate difficult things.

Shame is something people often project onto themselves without ever even realizing that is what they are doing. If you're someone who stays quiet when you're upset because you think it will make the other person angry or uncomfortable, you are shaming yourself for having thoughts and feelings. If your internal dialogue is negative and you tell yourself often things like, you should have done better, you're so fat, you're so pathetic, you screwed up again, those are all statements rooted in shame that your brain is listening to, and taking feverish notes about who you are.

Think about it this way, if your friend has a goal to lose 50 pounds, and every day you look at them when you see them and say, "you're fat and ugly and this is why you're still single," how long do you think that friendship would last, and furthermore how motivating is that really?

Now think about that same friend and every day you saw them you said, " Hey! I know you're not where you want to be, but you will get there and are doing great!" Sound better? I hope so! Now I want you to stop and think about how you talk to yourself. Is it more like the first statement or the second? What I tend to come across in my work is that most of us talk to ourselves the first way. We tend to motivate through shame, and all that does is drive you deeper into a low place that makes it near impossible to get out of. Be honest with yourself and think about how you speak to yourself. Sarcasm and making fun of yourself is also considered shame, by the way. For every negative thing you say about yourself, you must remember that your brain is listening and taking notes. If you're not careful and all or most of the notes are negative and shameful, that is the identity you will start to believe in. You will start to believe you are what you tell yourself you are, so it is imperative that you lead with love and speak to yourself in such a manner.

If you find that your internal dialogue is on more of the negative side, then it's an indicator somewhere along the way you veered off the path of being connected to your worth. Being connected to your worth means you are also mindful of how you are motivating yourself. You can hold yourself accountable and do hard things, but lead with love, encouragement, and support, not shame and insults. Meeting yourself with compassion and softness doesn't mean you can't hold yourself accountable and do hard things, it just means you cheer yourself on throughout the process rather than emotionally abuse yourself.

When you are consistently shaming yourself, often times without even realizing it, you are creating a pattern of getting comfortable feeling less than and hiding behind that shame while comparing yourself to others. You are settling, in a sense for half a life. Sometimes shaming yourself is a coping skill you picked up along the way to hide from potential failure. If you don't try then you can't fail, right? That's half a life. Failing is part of the dance and it allows you an opportunity to find out what you like, what you don't like, and who YOU are as a person, not who everyone thinks you should be.

I remember when my marriage ended in my late twenties and I was feeling happy to be out on one hand, but also really unsure of ever finding something that was healthy. I was so hard on myself about marrying him in the first place, that almost daily I would shame and blame myself for not being where I thought I should be by now in life. I can remember having second thoughts and not trusting my gut to get out of the marriage, but I married him anyway, and man did I punish myself for that for a couple of years both in and out of the marriage. There were countless nights he just wouldn't come home or show up when he said he would. Sound familiar? He was the emotional carbon copy of my biological father. I tell people often and whole heartedly believe, that if we aren't careful many of us end up marrying our unfinished emotional business. It's our unfinished emotional business that ends up hurting us more than the outward physical behavior most of the time. I knew that I didn't want to marry someone who physically hit like my father did, but I didn't understand yet, that it's the emotional trauma that happens day in and day out on a subconscious level that we end up repeating if we are not careful. The unhealthy emotional patterns are what we end up repeating most, because as children our brains start to take pride in learning how to protect us, and in a sense start to feel at home when they are triggered by familiar albeit unhealthy patterns. When I call it unfinished, I mean that we haven't acknowledged the pattern and how we participate in it. In my case, I hadn't acknowledged this type of behavior as a deal breaker. I hadn't learned to connect to my worth and value, and was still stuck in the loop of jumping into fix it mode and putting my worth in other people's hands.

It took me a bit to make the connection, but I can remember feeling like the way to be loved and accepted was to be strong and just do everything for the house and marriage myself. It's like we lived separate lives on many levels, and I though being strong just meant take responsibility for the choice I had made to marry him and moving forward. He had a terrible alcohol problem, and left me feeling less than and lonely on too many occasions to count. He also had an uncanny ability to make me feel like if I was more fun, prettier, or better to be around then maybe he would come home.

Enter five year old Lisa whose emotional memory was strong and for a while tried harder to be picked, and personalized everything. I can remember exhausting myself that first year of marriage trying to be all that he kept telling me I wasn't. About two years into the marriage I was emotionally exhausted and lower than I had ever been. The story I was telling myself and those around us, was one full of shame and mistruths. I minimized his drinking and covered for him, so people would't know I married a guy who didn't want to be around me. I told myself often that I didn't need anybody and could do everything on my own and would, which wasn't true. I wanted somebody. I wanted a partner and a healthy marriage but the trouble was that it was only me showing up to the marriage. The pendulum would swing and I would say things like, maybe I'm too strong and if I needed him more he would come home, or maybe I am too outspoken and if I talked less he would want to come home. Maybe if I drank and partied more he would invite me to do things. It breaks my heart just writing this, thinking about this frantic young woman being controlled by her five year old inner child, just trying everything she knew how to do to be loved.

I remember about four years into the marriage, I kept thinking about leaving but always stopped myself and said I don't want to give up on him. One day though, I woke up and the house smelled like vomit, there was liquor and beer cans everywhere and he was passed out in the spare bedroom. I remember walking through the mudroom to the car to go to work and thinking, wait a minute, I am giving up on me by staying. The story I've been telling myself about how its all my fault and I am too this or too that is just not true. He chooses to drink, cheat, and lie. He isn't choosing me, but rather is always choosing himself, why aren't I?!

It was in that moment I knew I was done. While something happened that day and I called myself out for telling a story that didn't serve me, but rather enabled him, it was a couple of more years until I put all of the pieces together and started to tell a story that portrayed who I was, and what I wanted. It was a few months after that realization that I left and served him with divorce papers. I put a lot of money and time into the home we purchased and can remember telling myself often during the marriage, if I ever leave him I will get this house, and all of the things I had worked so hard for. In the end, when it came right down to it, I didn't want anything that was associated with him. My lawyer encouraged me to ask for more and hold him accountable financially, but I just didn't want to. It wasn't out of fear, it was because for the first time in a long time, I was choosing what felt right to me no matter what everyone else thought I should do. The things I thought I wanted turned out the be just things, and while it would have been nice to have been compensated for everything I supported him with throughout the marriage, I prioritized my freedom and mental health over that. I didn't want to be tied to him in any way.

I started holding myself accountable for making empowered choices, understanding what I was feeling and asking for what I needed. A lot of this started to change for me, when I met myself with compassion for what I had been through and dropped the shame and anger. When I looked inward and asked why, I started to figure out the why not. I started to figure out why I didn't want to tell that story anymore and connected to my value and my worth. Somedays it was one thought or choice that chose me, and other days it was multiple. I started small and let the veil of shame slowly lift until one day I not only knew who I was and what I wanted, but took full accountability for my role and my story that wasn't working. If I had let my shame lead, I think I probably would have drug him through court to get the money he owed me, so I could tell myself it wasn't all for not, and so other people would see me as strong. For the first time in a long time though, I saw myself as strong and that was enough for me.

I started telling myself a story that included, who I was proud to be, what I had learned from the past and a story that included what I wanted. Rather than saying things like, I'm too strong men are intimated by me, nobody will want a divorced girl, I'll never have kids because I missed my chance, I started saying things like, I am proud of being strong and the right person is going to value that, being divorced is a part of my story and a part of life, I own it and will not shame myself for it. I met the negative limiting aspects of my narrative with compassion and started to fall in love not only with who I was, but also with the unknown. I started to connect to what I needed and dropped the need to control how it happened. I focused on making choices that were becoming of me and my worth.

That approach changed everything for me. It allowed me work on the person I was proud of being and relish in that. It stopped me from hiding behind a story that just wasn't true and was full of excuses to not change and grow. That was the beginning on my growth journey. There was a part of me, that was excited to discover and love all of the new ways I had found to navigate the world, but I didn't stop to think how this would all feel when put into practice. I mean sure, it was exciting to sit in my cozy house in the mountains and find a new love for myself and zest for life, but what I wasn't anticipating was how often things would get tested, and how easy it was to slip into old habits as a subconscious default of sorts to keep myself safe.

Starting today, I am going to challenge you to be aware of your internal dialogue. Your internal dialogue is that little voice that chimes in throughout the day. How you speak to yourself matters and is the foundation from which your narrative and story are created. Just pay attention to how often that dialogue is limiting, negative, or shameful. I have a feeling most of you will be surprised how automatic that negative voice has become. When you catch it, start to re direct it, and meet yourself with positive support, accountability and compassion.

Telling an authentic story and living an authentic life, means looking back on where you've been and getting brutally honest with yourself about where the story started to change to one in which you kept yourself stuck with limiting beliefs. The story you tell the world matters, but the story you tell yourself is what matters most. Don't ever underestimate how powerful words are. The words we speak to ourselves and others and the words we hear from the people we invite into our life, all matter.

For example, if you grew up in a house that didn't acknowledge your wants and needs, and wasn't good at talking about feelings, then it's possible you learned that your wants, needs, and feelings don't matter. To stay safe you stopped verbalizing them as a child, especially if they were met with hostility and dismissiveness. Now, as an adult you let everyone know you're just a go with flow kind of person and don't really have an opinion on much, or you shame yourself for having an opinion and speaking your mind. If that's the truth and you made that choice for yourself, that's fine, but if that story came from never feeling validated and leaves you feeling like nobody notices you, then the new story needs to be, I am learning how to speak up and try new things. My wants and needs do matter, I'm just not very good at articulating them yet. See the difference?

I'll do one more, then you can try. If your story is that you'll be single forever and there are no good guys out there because maybe you were hurt in the past and afraid to trust, then own that. Acknowledge what happened in the past, give yourself some compassion for it, and change the story to a more authentic one. The new one here might be, I'm single right now, but I'm doing the work on me be ready for the right guy when I meet him. I've been hurt in the past, but still want to find my person.

Assignment #2

Take some time and think back to your childhood, previous relationship, or any other previously difficult time in your life. How did you cope with that situation? Start to write down where you may have started to disconnect from feeling worthy and where that internal dialogue started to change to one full of limiting mis truths. Write down what was happening and how you compensated or coped with that.

Then in your journal, write down things you are currently shaming yourself about and how that is effecting your narrative. For each item, write an acceptance statement to counteract that shame. IE I am too weak and never speak my mind = Shame. The acceptance statement should read: I was never validated as a child and made to feel stupid if I brought up my feelings. That has carried with me into adulthood, but I know now that my thoughts feelings and emotions do matter.

I was never any good at relationships, so it's no surprise I am in a bad one now = shame. The new acceptance statement should read, My pattern in the past is to choose people who are immature and unavailable, I know

now, that it could be a sign I need to choose myself first and become

connected to me.

Chapter 3

What is a Mistake, if Not an Opportunity

Mistakes are inevitable. We've all heard the term, nobody is

perfect, and that statement is in fact true. In life, when we make a mistake

we have two choices: Shame and blame or get curious about yourself and

others. Curiosity means you are open to asking yourself, *why* you did

something rather than just shaming yourself and beating yourself up for it.

Shame and blame does not equal accountability contrary to popular belief.

Shame and blame only keeps you stuck in the hole you've dug and doesn't

allow you any traction to get out. Accountability is important, but more so,

is how you enact that accountability. Accountability means taking ownership of your part in the problem, and meeting yourself with compassion as you do. Accountability means being responsible for yourself and being mindful of those around you.

Meeting yourself with curiosity and compassion after a mistake allows you the traction to move forward using that experience as knowledge to change things and do better. Shaming only puts a heavier pressure on you to disconnect from your worth and value. Turning that energy inward and learning about yourself is one way to create a self identity that helps you feel prideful and empowered. Creating a self identify in which you are proud of and connected to means committing to learn about yourself, what you need, how you operate best, and what's important to you. What you are going to realize, when you make the commitment to understand and know yourself, is that things that may have seemed like red flags before, will now be deal breakers and the clarity that you are able to approach and engage others with is crystal clear.

I have met numerous clients over the course of my career who's worth is dependent on being perfect or being perceived as perfect. When they make a mistake or unintentionally hurt someone their default behavior is to get defensive and protect themselves. They have placed so much of their worth and value on external factors and people's perception, that they haven't allowed a space to be human and take accountability in an effort to learn about themselves and others. Often times these people when met with feedback or critics, turn to a defensive posture, because their value in this world is literally dependent on being seen as perfect.

When I work with clients like this, the first question I often ask is what scares them the most about making a mistake? The answers typically range from things like people thinking I am incompetent, making someone else mad or disappointed, or feeling like a failure. Notice that these are all external forces driving their need for perceived perfection.

When we can make a mistake and use it to invite self compassion in, we allow ourselves the emotional space to be human and foster an environment of curiosity and improvement. When you are constantly fighting to defend a notion of perceived perfection, your focus is solely on keeping up appearances which is neither authentic or an easy place to exist. Having compassion for yourself or the version of yourself from the past that made mistakes is the first step in creating a space and identity that is comfortable and empowering to live in.

I had a client in her forties who came to my office every week to work on anxiety and people pleasing tendencies. We did a lot of work regarding owning her own wants and needs and not being afraid to verbalize them. We worked through challenges and fears that she had with doing so, by reframing the fear into a "what if it works out" scenario. So, rather than assuming that a conversation would go badly, I challenged her to start to look at the ways it could go well. We challenged her catastrophic thinking, we validated her wants and needs, we talked about her co workers and their communication style, and we looked at this thing from just about every angle I could think of. We did this for a few months with little to no change. Until one day, something changed and we had a break through.

She came into my office one day, quiet, soft, and reserved as usual, but today instead of sitting and waiting for me to start the session, she started and asked me why she couldn't get the courage to speak up for herself? She was terrified and convinced that she was destined to live a life for others and what they needed. When I asked what she thought the payoff was for her always doing what others wanted even if it hurt her, she began crying. She cried for a few minutes, slumped over in her chair, Kleenex over her face, and I let her. I knew what was coming and knew she needed to get this out, so I created a space of safety and quiet for her to cry. After those few minutes, she looked up at me and quietly squeaked out, "why?" On the verge of tears myself, I sat forward in my chair and looked into her eyes for a moment. I had really come to adore this client, and would root for her often. I knew there was more in there, but she hadn't felt ready to share, so until she was I kept things pretty surface level when it came to her sessions.

I slanted my head to the left and gave her a compassionate look of, it's ok you can tell me, and then I asked her, "What exactly is it you are punishing yourself for?"

The tears started again, but this time were accompanied by a huge exhale as she slumped lower into her chair. I waited a few moments and let her continue to cry, and was grateful on one hand she felt safe enough to do so and heartbroken on the other hand that it had taken a little over two months for her to feel safe enough to do so. I had a feeling that her feeling safe enough to be vulnerable with anyone was a big deal, and this wasn't something I took lightly.

Through the tears, she went on to tell me that in college she turned to drinking alcohol to fit in and feel more comfortable in social situations. She recounted the first time she drank also being the first time in her life that she felt she was seen by others as something other than "ordinary." She went on to tell me that she would feel so terrible about herself the morning after and was so ashamed of the choices she was making, but then again when a social situation arose, she would drink.

Because of her drinking she had put herself in some situations where she didn't behave kindly to herself or others. Although, she was able to stop drinking, she never asked herself the real reason she started to begin with. Her need to be liked and to feel worthy outweighed what she knew in her gut was right. So here she sat in my office, in her mid forties scared to death of feeling like a lonely young woman in college again, so instead of drinking to be liked, she started minimizing herself and just saying yes to everything in an effort to be liked an accepted.

As our sessions went on, we were able to uncover that she carried a great deal of shame over the mistakes of her past, and even realized that her past felt so shameful, that she thought all she deserved today was what people would give her. She felt that the neglect and negative behavior from others that she experienced on a daily basis was penance for how she had treated people and herself in college.

Sitting across from her in the softest voice I could muster, I asked if she felt any compassion for a young woman dying for acceptance so much that she felt like she had to make those choices with alcohol to be liked and to fit it in. Through tears she shook her head no.

I went back even further and asked her if she felt any compassion for her ten year old self that was often times dismissed and neglected by her parents, she slowly shook her head yes.

There it was. She saw mistakes as a reflection of her worth and place in this world. She had a ten year old dancing around her heart trying to run an adults life. That ten year old had learned that she didn't really matter, and that what mattered more were people and things going on around her. When she felt dismissed as a child, she turned inward and shutdown. When she felt dismissed as a young adult, she turned to alcohol to combat that feeling, and then shamed herself for her mistakes daily.

When we were able to uncover why she made the mistakes she did, we were able to work through seeing them as less of an indicator of her worth, and more of an indicator of the coping skills she picked up in childhood. We worked together to go back and give that little girl all of the love, support and validation she was so worthy of and didn't get. After working through and loving her ten year old self, we were able to move to her twenty year old self and then keep that momentum going into her mid forties self. Every time she caught herself choosing to just accept what people would give her, she could validate that inner child and remind herself that she matters and is more than enough for herself and for those around her. In a sense, she became the person she needed as a child and didn't get.

That my friends is how mistakes snowball into a pattern of shame before you even realize what is happening. When you can understand why you make the choices you make, it often times gives you the information you need to go inward and change the pattern. This wasn't about erasing mistakes from this clients past or blaming her parents for something, this was about forgiving herself and giving herself a soft place to land and then jump from to change the future.

Most mistakes in life happen on a smaller scale and happen everyday. Sometimes they are mindless slips when there is too much on your plate or sometimes they are just choices you make that you thought were the right ones at the time. Either way, the process is the same for moving through them. Meet yourself with compassion, ask yourself why, learn from them and let them go. Mistakes don't define you in a negative light unless you let them. They have an opportunity to define you in a positive empowered light if you drop the need to be perfect and adopt the honor of being human.

It is okay and a part of life to be in disappointed in yourself at times when things don't work out how you intended. That disappointment is yet another indicator to be accountable to moving through something and moving forward. It's ok to be angry, disappointed, embarrassed or confused, just challenge yourself to not stay stuck there. Staying in one place while life happens around you just keeps you further down in a hole, with all the good stuff happening around you, just waiting for you to get out of your hole and take part.

Assignment #3

Grab your journal and write down the things from your past or even just yesterday that you are holding onto and not forgiving yourself for. Soften your approach, by taking a deep breath and releasing the tension from your body, and then write down what you can learn from those mistakes. Offer the younger version of you compassion for what you went through, and then reframe that mistake by deciding how you will use it in the present to break old patterns and make different choices. Remember to connect to your worth and value as you do this exercise. Moving forward, if you find yourself punishing yourself for mistakes that you make, or mistakes for your past, use them as an indicator to offer love and validation to your current self to move forward empowered and softer. Remind yourself it's ok to be human and you're ok. You don't have to be perfect to be worthy.

Chapter 4

Why Me?

Before we move on to boundaries and teaching people how to treat you, I want to remind you about cultivating a relationship with your self worth. Remember, this is not something you have to earn, it's something you were born with and got disconnected from along the way. Cultivating a connection with your self worth, means showing up everyday and connecting with it. Think of it this way, if you're in a relationship, do you show up every 6 months or so and check in with that person for a minute then leave and expect that to be a relationship that grows long term? I hope not! Cultivating a relationship with your worth works the same way. You can't show up every six months or so and expect to stay connected to yourself. You have to show up everyday and remind yourself that you are worthy, you bring value to this world, and are capable of hard things.

I can't begin to tell you how many times I have explained this concept to clients in what I believe to be this beautiful, soft but direct delivery, and just when I think they are getting it, I swear I can hear a record screech to a halt somewhere when they ask me, "So, how do I do that?"

I tell them one thing, and that is accountability. You have to make a conscious choice to be accountable to yourself and your worth everyday. In the beginning it might feel uncomfortable or even a little silly, but the more your brain gets used to the idea of loving and accepting you, the more automatic it becomes. Think about how you grow a romantic relationship. You get to know that person, you get excited about spending time with that person, you do nice things for that person and say nice things to that person. It's the same for connecting with yourself. You wake up every morning and say nice things to yourself, spend time with yourself, and do nice things for yourself. Every day.

When there are moments that don't feel good or put you in a place of shame, you have to challenge yourself to not give up on you, and take a breath and support yourself through the hard times. You become your own best friend and behave in a way that takes care of you. That means with both actions and words. Words matter, and how you speak to yourself especially during hard times, in my opinion matter most.

The reason self worth is so important when we are talking about boundaries and teaching people how to treat you, is that if you don't believe you're worthy of respectful nice treatment, either will anyone else. If you don't respect yourself other people won't know what you need and how you'd like to be treated.

The title for the book is actually quite personal to me, and has become somewhat of a joke with my friends and I. For quite a few years, before I met Jeff, I had what one could call a somewhat rocky relationship with the dating world. Men would ghost me, cheat on me, not show up when they say they would and just do some pretty crappy things. I would call my best friend Airika, and tell her of my latest woes, and she would say something supportive but brutally honest like, "Ugh, sorry buddy, he turned out to be a real ass." To which I would always reply, "It's great, it's fine, I'm fine." Which was really just a default response to anything bad that was happening in my life. The truth was, that it wasn't fine! I was frustrated, hurt, and sometimes just downright angry. I think I said it so often that it really did become a joke after a while.

While at some point we were able to start laughing about how ridiculous my dating life had become, I said it when anything bad happened. My landlord raised my rent one year and I had no idea how I was going to be able to afford it, but eh it's fine! No it wasn't. My job that I was doing at the time allowed me to work from home, and then decided it wanted me to start driving an hour into their office every week, but it's fine! No, it wasn't. Boyfriend and I broke up and he was scary enough to have to take out a restraining order, meh just fine. No, it definitely wasn't.

The pattern I am trying to establish here for you, is that sometimes things aren't fine and not acknowledging that is not strength, it's dismissive of you and your feelings. In many ways not acknowledging what hurt you or what is troubling you, gives that other person a free pass to keep treating you in a way that doesn't feel good. In life, we get the results we think we deserve. How do we generate better results? Step one is knowing you're worth it. Step two is understanding that acknowledging things and working through them, provides you an opportunity to actually explore how you're feeling and decide what you need to resolve it. Step three is committing to the idea that boundaries aren't meant to keep people out of your life, they are meant to keep people in your life, in a healthy way that feels good to both of you.

Often times, I hear clients tell me that they are afraid of setting boundaries or speaking up for themselves because of how the other person might react. They fear that the other person's reaction will make them feel like they are difficult or mean, and rather than face the other persons reaction they stay silent and accept whatever they are given. The first thing we need to get to the root of here, is why they are attempting to manage the other person's reaction to their boundary. It is not your job to manage the other person's reaction to your boundaries. It is your job to connect to yourself and understand and acknowledge how you're feeling and what you need. If you deliver this message to someone, using an approach that is becoming of your worth, ie not angry or forceful, then what you have done is give another person a road map regarding how you wish to be treated.

If that other's person's reaction is disrespectful or angry, then I can make a pretty solid guess that they don't respect themselves and so it will be near impossible for them to respect you.

I'll give you an example. Earlier in this chapter I made mention of an ex boyfriend who I took an order of protection out on. Early on in our dating relationship, I was still working in an emergency department, which could be stressful and include quite a few long days. For our second date, the plan was for me to leave work and drive 45 minutes to his house. It was nearing the end of my day, and we had a trauma come in. It was a little boy who had hurt himself quite badly in a biking accident. His mother was obviously distraught and not doing well. My job when these things happened was to offer support to the family and keep them informed of what was going on. This particular case was a difficult one, and wasn't going to wrap up anytime soon. I called this person who I was supposed to go out with, to let him know I wasn't going to make it that night. I explained that I just felt like I wanted to go home and decompress alone. I told him how I was feeling and what I needed, in a calm way.

His response, looking back was a huge red flag, and was an angered one. He made it about him and the night he had planned, and was angry with me for ruining that. I was so exhausted from the day, I didn't even really know how to respond and actually ended up feeling bad. If that wasn't enough, when I told him I needed to just have some alone time, but I was up for rescheduling our second date, yes second date, he took it upon himself to serial text me, all night until I finally shut my phone off. Even writing this, I cringe at that fact that I didn't just end things with him right there, but looking back I was able to learn from it, and take people pushing back on my boundaries much more seriously now.

That kind of pattern continued over the course of our relationship. There were times, when he would get angry or frustrated with me, and my default was to always try to fix it. This time was a bit different though, because I knew by the pit in my stomach and the way I fell so far our of alignment with myself to be with him, that this relationship had no future. When I broke up with this person about two months in, of course he couldn't respect a boundary, and ended up pushing it to the point of me feeling unsafe. He would call from multiple numbers, sent letters to my house and to my place of employment, and would do things like send me pictures of him with an outline of a person next to him that was supposed to be me. It was unsettling to say the least. One day I asked a colleague and police officer, who I worked with sometimes in the emergency department to give him a call and ask him to leave me alone. I had asked several times for him to leave me alone, and hadn't responded to any of his attempts to communicate with me in weeks. When the colleague looked at everything he had sent to me and listened to all of the voicemails, he told me that he needed to go arrest him for stalking. I was shocked, and didn't expect things to escalate to that level. I certainly knew I was afraid and wanted him to leave me alone, but didn't think it would get to this. Before filing charges the officer called him and asked why he hadn't left me alone when I had made myself clear I wanted to no further contact with him. The ex told the officer, something to the effect of well, you know women you have to keep at it. My colleague's response was a stern one, in which he told him to leave me alone.

My colleague said, "Listen Lisa, if I am over reacting and don't have grounds to file these charges, then the district attorney and judge won't grant the warrant, but at this point he had a legal responsibility as a police officer to report this." Within two hours the judge not only granted the warrant but added a class 5 felony of stalking. It didn't end there, the ex's mother reached out to me telling me what a horrible person I am, and that I am ruining her son's life. I of course didn't reply but handed even more evidence over to the DA. I wanted it to all just go away and all I wanted was for him to leave me alone and to feel safe again. I didn't care if he got arrested or not, I just wanted a restraining order that protected me.

The district attorney saw things differently and felt strongly about pushing forward with the charges. It was hell for me, and probably one of the most terrifying and stressful times of my life. He ended up taking a deal that dropped the felony to a misdemeanor and I got a restraining order. He never contacted me again, thankfully!

At first, I started thinking to myself, why does this stuff always happen to me? It wasn't long before I realized I was asking myself the wrong question with him and countless others before him. The appropriate question should have been, Why do I continue to allow this? Looking back, I continued to allow a lot of things I shouldn't have, because I didn't think I deserved more or because I was afraid of someone's reaction if I ended things or set a boundary. I actually ended things with Mr. boundary pusher twice before the final time, because of his anger and how he treated others, scaring me. He would beg and plead and tell me that wasn't the real him, and he was just stressed and would do better, so when I started feel guilty for choosing me, I would give him another chance. I didn't ask for what I needed, for fear of that person leaving and not choosing me, or better yet them being disappointed or hurt.

As I result I stayed in places and situations for longer than I should have because of my attempt to manage their emotions rather than connect to mine. I put myself in a lot of situations where nobody was choosing me, not even me. Some may look at Mr. boundary pusher and say he wanted to spend time with you, he was choosing you, and to that I say, no he wasn't. He was choosing his agenda and what he wanted over respecting me and my boundaries, and taking accountability for himself. Choosing me, would have looked like him saying something like, "Woah that sounds like a really hard day, I am disappointed, but let me know when we could reschedule, I'd love to see you again." Or, maybe " I don't want to end things, but I get that you want to." Do you see the difference?

In an ideal world relationships both romantic and not romantic would all be 100/100. Meaning, that each person brings some sense of their best selves to the table. This would allow all of us to be in touch with who we are and what we need and be able to communicate that to each other. In a sense we would all just draw each other a road map of what we need and on the flip side of that we would be able to also know how to respect and treat others. Unfortunately, that's more often than not how it works. We are all human with different stories, wants, needs and dreams. How we communicate and navigate the world is all different as well. If you meet someone and there is a wide disconnect on say values, then they may not be a bad person, just not someone you will invest a lot of time in and that's ok.

I think that most of us know on some level the kind of relationship we would like to have with others, but what we have an opportunity to realize, is that we must first create this relationship with ourselves. It isn't boundaries we struggle with as much as it is letting go of the need to control or feel responsible for someones else's emotions and opinions. You simply must let go of the notion that you are responsible for someone else, there is no way to honor yourself and and be responsible for others at the same time. Often times, this type of thinking is so engrained in us and how we relate to relationships, that we create a large space of discomfort when we think about honoring ourselves first. I promise you, that if you are self abandoning to be chosen by others, it is the greatest indicator in the world that it's time to choose yourself.

Boundaries are difficult for a lot of us, but also necessary. If you struggle with setting boundaries, remember they don't have to be angry or forceful. Boundaries can be communicated in a loving and soft way. I've created an acronym for you to remember and use to practice setting boundaries.

T - Teach people how to treat you

A - Acknowledge how you feel and what you need.

L - Let the other person know

K - Kick the habit of managing other people's reactions to your boundaries

Example: Hey, I get that you are angry, but your tone is making me feel uncomfortable, so if you want to talk about this, I am happy to do so, but it needs to be done calmly. If you're not in a calm space we can table this for when you are.

Example: I really love it when you visit, but I do better with a bit of a heads up so I can focus on you and our visit, not all the things I have to do around the house. Could you call before coming over to make sure I'm in a good place for a visit?

Assignment # 4

Grab your journal and write down which relationships in your life feel like they could use some boundaries. Write down what's bothering you, what are you feeling and what you need from this other person? Empower yourself to know that you are allowed to teach people how to treat you. Boundaries don't have to be angry, they can be soft and thoughtful of the others's persons emotions, but not an attempt to control them. Write down examples of what you might say to this person to set the boundary, and practice if you're nervous!

Extra Credit: Think about boundaries people have set with you and write down where you may have some opportunities to meet and respect those boundaries and not personalize them as a reflection of your worth or value to them.

Chapter 5

Change Your Relationship to Your Feelings, but Leave your Feelings

Alone

Let me be clear, every single feeling you feel is valid, but is most

certainly not fact. Feelings are like visitors, you have to let them come in

before they will leave. I don't want you to ever think you have to change

how you feel, but I do want to remind you that what matters most is *what*

you choose you to do with them.

When we think about negative emotions like sadness, loneliness,

and anger, I find that more often than not people come to me and say I don't want to feel this way anymore. My response is always the same, you will feel that way until you decide what you want to do with it. It's not about just making the emotion go away, it's about learning what it's trying to tell you about yourself and what you need.

So, what if for a moment you stopped trying to push emotions away and you let them in to a judgment free zone and used them as markers for getting to know and getting connected to yourself. Your feelings are the roadmap to learning about yourself, and if you refuse to let any emotion in or only certain ones, you will never really know yourself. Filtering feelings has an adverse snowball effect that directly effects the relationship you have with yourself.

Often times people think that there is something wrong with them for having maybe too many emotions, too intense emotions, or confusing emotions, so rather than pushing and exploring them they block them out and push them down. They minimize themselves and prioritize a perceived comfort in the moment of not feeling anything negative. Not exploring your emotions, makes it truly impossible to start to understand them, which means that you will stunt the learning process of getting to know yourself. If you don't know yourself on a deeply connected level how on earth will you ever really know what your values are and what's important to you? If you don't know what your values are then you can't

possibly commit to living an authentic life based on your value system and

self identity, and if you can't do that for yourself then who's life are you

living? Phew, what a snowball effect!

Do you see the problem I am outlining with minimizing and not

exploring your emotions? We live in a society where emotions tend to

scare people usually because they don't know what to do with them, so

they tend to make us uncomfortable. When we are uncomfortable often

times we think we need to get out of the situation, but in this case I am

challenging you to push trough that discomfort and get curious about what

your emotions are telling you about yourself.

Pushing them down and ignoring them, or pretending they aren't

there isn't a healthy approach and only causes more pain in the long run.

Letting your emotions come in and then deciding what you'd like to do

with them is the first step to getting comfortable with your own emotions.

Emotions are clues about who you are, and while they aren't all fact there

is most definitely always a reason you feel what you feel.

Theres another term we hear a lot these days and that is toxic

positivity. Toxic positivity is a term used for people that don't want to

acknowledge and explore their negative emotions, so they mask everything with a positive spin. I am all for reframing and looking on the bright side, but there's a consequence to ignoring your negative feelings and just masking them with a positive spin. Doing this doesn't allow you to process and resolve the negative feeling, but rather just throw some dirt and flowers on it, and call it good. That may work for a while, but sooner or later that weed will show its ugly head and take over.

Clinical research shows that when you try to deny an emotion you actually end up feeling it more intensely. Most of us have been taught from a young age to block and avoid our emotions rather than deal with them. A lot of us do it quite well and self medicate with things like our phones, substance use or isolating. Your emotions are biological forces that should not be ignored and are there to help you survive. When you push emotions away it puts stress on your mind and your body which creates a psychological distress and can manifest in a multitude of physical symptoms. Neurological research shows the more emotions and conflicts a person experiences the more anxiety they tend to feel. The emotional center of your body responds to your emotions and sends signals to you lungs, your heart and your intestines, which readies your body to take action to survive. In short, your emotions actually aren't a part of your conscious control, and you can't actually stop them from being triggered. Understanding this concept can help you create a space to not judge your emotions and push them down, but rather allow yourself to feel them and get curious about why you are feeling what you're feeling.

When you can identify your emotions and allow them in, you are able to deepen the connection you are building with yourself and have a better understanding of who you are. Allowing your emotions in, in a judgement free space also allows you an objective space to decide what you want to do with them. For example, if you're feeling shame or embarrassment, rather than judging it or sucking it up, you can create a space to give yourself compassion and support. Creating a safe space to get curious about why you are feeling something, allows you start to make sense of them. The other consequence of suppressing or pushing emotions down, is that they don't go away on their own and stay there until you deal with them. The more you suppress the more you disconnect from what you need and who you are. Not knowing what you need or who you are anymore, means you start to live for other people and not for yourself. In a sense you are living half a life and getting more and more disconnected from who you are, which in my experience typically leads people to feeling alone and resentful in.

I had a client once who would come into my office each week and talk to me about not feeling like he was able to say how he was feeling at home, so he would push it down to the point he would explode in anger and say things he didn't mean. This caused major ramifications and hurt in his relationship to say the least. We talked a lot about his anger and where it was coming from, but often times he wasn't able to actually say that it was his partner he was angry with. He was struggling a great deal with why he exploded on his partner and not coworkers, friends etc.

We worked for a while on being able to identify his emotions and attach a need to them, which he was able to with some consistency. I found more often than not in my work with him, that he could and would verbalize how he was feeling, but then explain it away and say things like, "that's not even a big deal, it shouldn't make me so angry." If we were looking at just that one screenshot in time, perhaps that one thing wasn't that big of deal, but when stacked upon layers and layers of other things he pushed down, that one little thing was the biggest deal and caused him to lose his temper.

Then one day, I asked him to draw me a map. I asked him to draw me a map that he could show his family where to go and how to get to the most authentic version of himself, the version he wanted be. After sitting for a few moments, he looked at me and said, "I don't even know where to start." It was in this moment I realized that he was hoping his partner would validate all of these feelings he wasn't communicating, but he himself didn't even know anymore how to validate his own feelings. He had pushed things down for so long, that he couldn't even draw a map or make a list of things he needed to feel validated and heard. I looked at him and said, "maybe it's harder than you think for someone to validate you and make your needs a priority if you yourself can't even tell me what they are."

As we worked through his needs and challenged him to start to speak up at home, slowly but surely this misalignment of character started to align itself. Slowly but surely he learned how to validate himself and his own wants and needs, and knew that the needs he couldn't meet for himself, were needs that he could challenge himself to talk to his partner about. While uncomfortable for him at first, his partner was thrilled that there started to be an emotional road map drawn regarding how to make him feel valid and secure in the relationship, a win win if you ask me. This wasn't a situation of his partner not caring what he wanted, this was a situation of his partner having no idea what he wanted, so she would do everything she thought he might need and was rarely right. When she had some direction, she could easily help him feel valid. Then she was able to start asking for and communicating things that she wanted and needed. When each person was responsible for themselves and what they needed, they could come to the table and work together to meet those needs.

Negative emotions not dealt with can breed negative patterns before you know it. In the therapy world, we refer to the term emotional reasoning when someone feels something and then cements it and makes it fact. They think, I feel it therefore I am it. Be careful with this type of pattern. While you can validate the feeling, challenge yourself to not cement it. Ask yourself do I really believe this or am I just feeling it?

Another negative emotional pattern that people tend to gloss over is what I call "shoulding" yourself. You make statements like I shouldn't have done that, I should really be doing this instead. Challenge yourself to start to speak in absolutes, and use statements like I can do this, I didn't do that, I will do this next time. I always say that should and shouldn't are rooted in shame. Speaking in absolutes is going to help you take charge of what you want to do with your emotions. Don't bash yourself for not knowing what to do right away or making the wrong choice. Practice self compassion, and take charge of your own life.

Jumping to conclusions consistently and jumping to catastrophic outcome is the last negative emotional pattern I want you to be aware of before we move on. Jumping to conclusions and assuming you know how someone else is feeling is the start of a lot of hurt feelings and personalization of people's behavior. If you want to know how someone is feeling, and whether or not it has anything to do with you, then ask! Get in the habit of asking instead of assuming.

If you're someone who always thinks about the worst case scenario, you are letting fear control your decisions. Thinking about everything in regard to a catastrophe is setting you up to live in a constant fight or flight state of mind, always on the look out to protect yourself. Remember when I told you earlier that words matter? They really matter here. If you're someone who handles rejection by saying things like, I will never date again or all men are evil, then I want you to get self aware of how often you're doing this. You may feel like all men are evil, but the truth is, maybe just that one was and you're more upset with yourself for dating them than anything else. Words matter, remember your brain is always listening so be mindful of what you tell it in the conscious world. The other problem with jumping to the worst case scenario before thinking about what you'd like to do with the emotion you're feeling, is that it clouds your judgement and makes it near impossible to see other potential solutions to a problem. When you can take just a second and soften your approach, you'd be amazed at how many possible solutions you can all of a sudden see to your problem.

Assignment #5

Grab your journal and set a timer for twenty minutes at the end of everyday. Create a judgement free zone in your mind and recap your day in feelings rather than events. Write down how you felt throughout the day. For every negative emotion, read it out loud to yourself and write next to it if you believe that or just felt it, and then attempt to attach a need to it to resolve it.

IE I felt confused and angry when my coworker who usually talks to me all day didn't talk to me at all today, and now I feel like she is mad at me. Response: I don't know if she is mad at me, but I do know that how I felt was valid, and that it didn't feel good to be ignored. What I need to do is reach out and ask how she is doing, and mention that she seemed a bit off at work and that I wanted to check in to see if everything is ok.

Odds are you'll find out her behavior had nothing to do with you, but in the case you did do something to upset her, this gives you an opportunity to take accountability and resolve it together.

The last three minutes of your twenty minutes, I would like you to write a love note to yourself in just a few sentences.

IE I love you, and am so proud of all that you are doing to get closer with yourself. You deserve rest sleep well.

Chapter 6

The Dreaded Timeline

I don't know about you guys, but it seems to me, like the pressure to be on

some imaginary timeline of success has gotten worse since social media

hit the scene. Social media gives everyone a glimpse into what you are or

aren't doing, and takes every opportunity it can to get you feeling like you

are boring, not enough, or in the wrong place.

I can vividly remember when I started to know that marrying my

ex husband was the wrong choice. I would push that feeling down and tell

myself that I am in mid twenties and don't want to start over. I even did the math once, and thought if I leave now, it might take 6 months to a year to meet someone, date for one to two years, get engaged and then get married. Oh ugh, I would be well into my early thirties by then, and then it would be too late. Too late for what??!! I actually had no idea, but had boxed myself into the imaginary timeline that I thought I needed to stay on to be successful. Lesson learned here was that I'd rather be with Mr. Right for the long haul rather than settle for Mr. Right now to fulfill some crap timeline society says we should be on.

I was so disconnected from my worth and what I wanted that I married him, and ended up divorcing him in my early thirties. Living an authentic life that feels good on the inside and doesn't just look good on the highlight reel of life, means falling in love with yourself and the unknown. It means training yourself to see the wonder and possibility in the unknown, not all of the what ifs and fear based scenarios. Looking back, yes I wish I wouldn't have married him and would have found my worth and value through travel or some other romantic way, but that is the choice I made. I married him, and then found my worth when I was ready to. I found it when it clicked with me that just surviving wasn't strength, but in fact was giving up on myself and living half of a life.

Social media, friends, and our society have a way of programming us from a young age to think that it's only the big things in life that matter. Things like, marriage, kids, travel, white picket fence etc, and yes those things are all wonderful, but they are just that, things. Those milestones and things or lack there of don't define your worth, you do. If those are things you want, then that's wonderful, but don't just go through the motions because you feel like you have to. A mantra I have adopted for myself and challenge all of my clients to also adopt, is " I don't have to, I get to." Not only is it rooted in gratitude, but it reminds you when you need it most that you are in charge of where your life goes. You are the one who goes to sleep at night feeling aligned or unaligned with your choices. If you find you are making choices out of fear for what others might think or how you will be judged by society, then odds are you are out of alignment, and that is not thriving, that is merely surviving.

If any of this resonated with you on some level, and you have built a life living in the what ifs and letting fear hold you back, I challenge you today, to start to ask yourself things like, what if it works out, what if I am happier, what if I start trusting my instincts and get to know myself and actually like myself? Those what ifs are full of wonder and possibility not fear and staying stuck.

Life is not meant to be easy and all a highlight reel, no matter what you see on social media or think others are doing. Life is a gift that all too often we turn into a race. If you're running that race for others, you'll never finish in a way that feels good. If you stop and treat life, like the gift it is, you'll find with most special things you'll want to take care of it. Adversity and trying new things are what affords you the opportunity to find out who you want to be. Take every opportunity you can. Push through discomfort and find out who you are.

After my divorce, I packed my jeep and one small U-haul trailer and headed west for Colorado. I had a job and a house lined up, but that's about it. I was lucky enough that my mom and step dad traveled often with us as kids out to the mountains to ski, and from a young age, I always remember feeling a sense of calm and home there. Living alone again was an adjustment, but one I was looking forward to. I was looking forward to only being responsible for me. I would wake up everyday and find new hikes, new activities and places to explore. I took every opportunity I had to push and try new things. Some things ended up teaching me what I didn't want, and other things captured my heart and inspired me to try again and make it part of my life.

One of the first hikes I did alone was a hike up to a glacier about an hour away from my house. I pulled into the parking lot and saw all of these people with backpacks and gear looking quite professional, and then glanced at what I had on and thought, oh wow I must be way under prepared here. At first I was intimated and thought I was going to look so silly trying to tackle this trail in my hiking shoes and carrying the one water bottle I had, while these people go up in their loaded packs, fancy sun hats and walking sticks. I sat for a second and thought to myself, I drove all the way here and I don't want to turn back without at least looking. I smiled when I passed other people, and found that the further along the trail I went the better I felt, and I even started to see some people who looked as prepared or ill prepared as I was. It turned out that I was judging the whole hike based on one group I saw in the parking lot, and when I pushed through my fear, realized I was just fine. I made it to the glacier and sat for a minute just looking at it. I remember feeling such a sense of pride and gratitude for having been brave enough to pick up and move in search of a place that felt like home. I felt the breeze blow softly on my face, and then I listened. I listened to the quiet, and for the first time in a long time felt like I was right where I needed to be.

There were definitely times that I felt so far off from what other thirty year olds were doing, that I felt behind. The pressure to have kids which is something I always wanted haunted me most. It was those moments, like the moments on the glacier, that taught me that right now is right on time, and this was my opportunity to learn to spend time with myself and to take care of myself in such a way that when I did meet the right person I would be ready to open my heart to them. How was anyone going to love me if I didn't even know how to really love myself yet.

That day was the start of an exploration of myself and my surroundings. It didn't just continue to go up and up, but rather the healing came in waves. Just as the hurt tends to happen in layers, so does the healing. I had many ups and many downs over the course of the next eight years. There were days I didn't think life could get any better, and then there were other days, I cried alone in my condo. I didn't know back then, how to meet myself with compassion, and it cost me a lot of lonely and sad nights, thinking I would never get to the elusive place, I thought I should be.

Then one day, when I was most definitely least expecting it, I walked into work for the first time in about two months. I had been off from work after having a knee surgery. I walked in and was so excited to see all of my co workers in the emergency department that I had missed, while I was away. My co workers will forever and always be family to me, whether they know it or not. They were hands down the best group I have ever worked with, and I really don't have the words to explain the difference that the love, support, and acceptance from them made in my life.There were many smiles all around as we all greeted each other, and then as I walked down the main corridor of the emergency department, I saw someone new, someone who I hadn't seen before.

It turned out, this person had started working there right around the time I left for my surgery. It's still not something I am very good at putting into words, but there was a sudden calm and a sense of intrigue when I saw him. There was a feeling of home for the second time in my life. I wasn't in a rush, I didn't have any anxiety, and I was 100 percent comfortable being myself and being curious about him.

Little did I know at the time, but eventually that man would become my best friend, and the man I fell in love with and share my life with today. He had a young daughter who would also become my everything, and a great deal of why I was brave enough to write this book and share some of my story. Watching her grow up and being lucky enough to be a part of it, reminds me often that learning to love, accept and respect ourselves is the greatest gift and strongest foundation from which we live. It also reminds me often, that when we can acknowledge and validate what we want in life, but stop the need to control how it happens, then you never know what might happen if you're brave enough to let it. I was thirty nine when I met Jeff and his daughter wasn't even two yet.

The work on myself didn't end there, and really in many ways had just begun. For so many years I had worked hard at staying connected to myself, and as happy as I was in my relationship, it was a challenge sometimes to stay connected to myself. The difference this time, was that I had found someone who encouraged me and supported my connection to myself. We cheered each other on, and supported one another being our best selves. When things got tough, we figured it out together.

Remember, our brains aren't wired to keep us happy they are wired to protect us, and learning how to stay connected to myself was key in making my relationship continue to grow. I had tried that before, and it never seemed to work, but the difference now, was that I had invited someone into my heart that wanted to take care of my story and support me being, well, me! The good news here is that I now knew who I was and what was important to me, so it was a natural thing to be able to verbalize those wants and needs to him, and allowed me the space to also be that person for him.

It is rarely the "big things" in life we have a problem imagining and hoping for, and it's the little in between moments we gloss over. In between moments, being all of the little things that make up our day to day lives, that happen in between the "big stuff" happening. When we gloss over the in between moments, and just focus on the big ones, we miss out on the opportunity to find joy and connection in them. Get curious, slow down and look for the little things that fill your heart up, because they are the moments that turn into the big ones, and they are the moments that remind you exactly how to connect to you and the world around you. It's in the small moments of life that we find gratitude and beauty. They are where we align with ourselves and our surroundings to take charge of the path we're on, not the path society tells us we should be on.

Assignment #6

Grab your journal and start thinking small. Think of small things that could turn into big momentum. Write down experiences or feelings that might seem insignificant but truly bring you joy. Maybe a morning cup of coffee in silence, maybe sitting in the sun and feeling the breeze on your face, a walk, reading a book… the list is full of possibilities. After you've made your list, seek those things out and be mindful of opportunities to experience them. When you do experience them, relish the moment, romanticize the moment. Doing this, will help to train your brain and your reward system to start to learn how much of this world and it's little in between moments that can connect you to yourself and fill you up. It's those in between moments that fill you up, so you have enough to give the others in your life. Seek them out, and don't ever apologize for things that make you happy, as these are the moments that keep you connected. What do YOU want out of life? Write it down, based on what YOU want, not what you think everyone else thinks you should want. Give it life, and make it a part of your story in your journal.

Chapter 7

Its not you, It's me

A very important term to get comfortable with before we put this all together is *accountability.* One of the questions I ask myself and my clients, is what is yours to take responsibility for or to be accountable for in this situation? I tend to get a lot of puzzled looks at first, but then I explain what I'm hoping for the client to gain by doing this exercise.

Navigating the world and relationships thinking that everyone else is the problem, is exactly that, the problem. While we can blame people for a lot of things, you always have a choice regarding what you choose to do with it, meaning you are accountable for what you do, what you learn and how you move through hard times. I firmly believe that in life, you don't treat people as bad as they are, but rather as good as you are. There will be some situations that you can honestly look at it and say I am not responsible for anything here other than how I get myself out of this situation. Sometimes, the only thing you need to choose to do with an experience, is make the choice to learn and move forward and apply your education to the next situation or relationship. Sticking around and waiting for an apology or closure, is not how you get accountable. Sticking around and waiting to blame someone else, is giving that other person way too much emotional real estate in your head and heart.

In most situations and relationships there is a space for accountability to be taken, to ensure you don't repeat that a pattern again. If your behavior caused hurt or pain, then maybe the accountability comes with the added task of apologizing and validating how your behavior has made someone feel. To say things like, if they hadn't done_____ I wouldn't have done _____ isn't creating a space of accountability and change but rather is just perpetuating blame. Remember, in life you will blame people for a lot of things that you had no control over, but you are 100 percent responsible for what you do with it. You don't treat people as bad as they are, you treat them as good as you are.

I can tell you for me, it took me a little while to realize my piece of the puzzle with my marriage. While it was true, I had nothing to do with fact that he was an alcoholic, nothing I could have said or done would ever warrant him emotionally abusing me, cheating me, or putting his hands on me, but still I was accountable for covering for him, enabling him out of fear for what he might do if he didn't have alcohol. I was accountable for allowing the behavior to happen to me, and not being clear about what my non negotiables were in the first place.

People in the community loved the fun outgoing guy he was, and had no idea what he was like behind closed doors. Often times out of embarrassment I would cover for him in public, make excuses when he didn't show up for work, or worse yet, tell my friends things that weren't even true in an effort to conceal what I had chosen for a marriage.

After the dust had settled on my divorce, I sent quite a few emails to people who over the years I wanted to apologize to for not telling the truth, and defending my ex husband even in the face of blatant wrong doing. When I left I remember telling myself that I had two choices. I could either save face with friends and the community and explain my side of the story or I could focus on rebuilding myself and getting out of an unhealthy place. I chose me. I chose me for the first time in a long time, and with that came consequences of some people getting extremely mad at me for leaving without warning to them. Now, my ex had all the warning in the world, but that is not of course what he was telling everyone in our small town.

He was really good at playing victim, and played to his strength here. To a lot of people in the community he was an injured little bird who needed comforting, and most people did just that. They comforted him, chose him and made sure to never talk to me again. I was blocked on social media, and had some friends just go silent it seems over night. The friends who wanted to know and took the time to ask what happened I absolutely took the time to tell them, but also never wanted to put anybody in a position to feel like they had to choose. In the years after I left, I had a few people reach out to tell me they were sorry for how they treated me when I left. What had happened since I left, was without me there to cover for him his true character presented itself.

It was a little over a year after I had left, and for some reason I found out that he was dating a woman, who I knew when we were married. I knew this woman to be a cheerful, intelligent woman who was always at community functions, so it didn't surprise me too much that she too had fallen for the victim plus I will show you the world act he was so good at putting out. I was a bit worried about her and thought about reaching out, but then stopped myself because I knew that just like me, nobody could have talked her out of being with him.

It wasn't long after that, one day while sitting on my balcony looking at the rocky mountains from my new condo, that I got a call from a mutual friend of both of ours. This friend hadn't talked to me since the divorce, but was calling to tell me that he had seen my ex's true colors and that it hadn't ended well with the woman that my ex was dating. It seems after me, he was actually sly enough to live some type of double life and was living with and dating two women at the same time, each with their own homes and own dogs! The difference this time, was that rather than leaving silently in the night, the woman that I knew he was dating spoke up and outed him for his behavior.

I remember feeling so sad for her, because on some level I knew the devastation of realizing you married a narcissistic drunk. I knew the feeling all too well, of knowing you are so much more intelligent than the choices you made, and the shame and confusion that came with that. I asked our friend for her number and asked if he thought it would be ok to reach out and offer my support.

I called her that evening and for the next few months we spent hours on the phone comparing notes, uncovering lies, and finding power in the future ahead. I was telling a co worker about this new friendship and they asked me, "Why would you do that and get involved again?" I paused for a moment and said, because I know now that what happened to me wasn't my fault, and if I had the opportunity to give someone else the gift of love and support I was going to take it. To this day, this woman and I cheer each other in the new chapters of our lives and console each other when we feel lonely or a bit disheartened with the world around us.

Not only did I get accountable to myself about what I would allow and the role I played in the marriage, but I took that and was able to turn it into a gift of clarity for someone else.

I learned that to effect real change and connect to my worth, I needed to take accountability for not only my actions, but also for the way I spoke to myself. As for the friends that chose to no longer talk to me, I also took accountability for respecting their need to cut me off. I was able to do this, because I didn't behave in a way that was intentionally hurtful to them, but rather behaved in a way that took care of me knowing that it may cause others to not want me in their life. I tried reaching out to one friend in particular to talk things through and see we if we could mend things between us, years later, but she wasn't willing. Ironically enough, she was friends with both women my ex later led the double wife with, so she knew he wasn't a great guy. I think what was different for me is that she didn't agree with or respect the fact that I left with little to no explanation.

While my intent was not to cause harm to others, my actions were a non negotiable for her, and that's something I have come to accept. Acceptance doesn't mean you agree or disagree with someone, it means you drop the need for a different outcome and work within the reality of the situation.

Just as we as humans sometimes seemingly fight daily to get people to respect our boundaries and wishes, there comes a time in everyone's life that you have the opportunity to do the same for someone else. If someone sets a boundary then you have an opportunity to respect that. It may not be what you were hoping for, but it's what is, and you can spend your energy trying to get someone to betray themselves and what they need or you can spend your energy reflecting on and accepting what they need. You don't have to agree with it, but I would challenge you to learn how to accept it.

The people who belong in your life will find their way back, this I have learned firsthand. As long as you behave in a way that is becoming of you and honors your value system, there is little left to say. It's not your job to manage other people and what they need, it is your job to navigate the world and relationships in a way that does no harm and keeps you connected to yourself. If you're thinking to yourself, I do that already but shouldn't the people around me who don't do that and cause harm be held accountable? The answer is, yes in a perfect world all people would be accountable for their actions and the consequence would fit the crime, but to take that on and make that your mission seems like an awful lot of misplaced energy to me.

Having a sense of what you need and what your deal breakers are, is what will guide you to make the choice of whether or not to invest in that relationship. If someone is mistreating you, you have two choices. First, talk to them about how their behavior makes you feel and come prepared with what you need from them to make it better. If you tell someone what you need and they say, sure no problem, then that's only the first step. The proof is in the pudding as they say, and then you watch for the action. If there is no action then they either aren't willing or aren't able to meet your need, no matter how well intentioned they are. At this point you are accountable to you, and deciding what you'd like to do next. Move on if the behavior is a deal breaker for you, or pull back on your investment. Either way, the choice is yours and yours alone, not theirs.

Often times, people say to me, but nobody is perfect and no relationship is perfect, so it's not that easy to just "give up". Let me be clear in saying, that I am not telling you to just "give up" I am challenging you to remember that relationships are two people working together to face the patterns and problems. Two people working together, each being accountable for themselves and how they show up to the relationship. If you are the only one showing up and trying, then all you're doing is giving up on yourself.

There will also be times that people come to you and let you know that you have hurt their feelings or done something they didn't like. This is not the time, as hard as it may seem, to get defensive. Most times people bring things to you to keep you in their life in a healthy way, not to push you out. If they didn't care they just would walk away. We tend to get defensive because it's natural to see someone's dislike with what you're doing as a reflection of how they feel about you, but I would challenge you to see it as a reflection of how they feel about themselves. Someone bringing something to your attention is a gift regarding insight on how they would like to be treated, and sometimes if we're open enough to listen it can strengthen your relationship and emotional connection with someone.

Assignment #7

Grab your journal and write down some of the things from your past that you blame other people for. Assign the blame to them and validate your pain, then write down what you'd like to do with it. How do you want that experience to change how you approach relationships, ask for what you need, set boundaries etc? After that, I want you to think about the role you played in that situation and look for ways that you could be accountable to yourself. Maybe it's how you shamed yourself, or blamed for yourself for the choices you were making. Maybe you enabled someone, maybe you stayed too long or didn't speak up for yourself. No matter what it is you find that you're accountable for, create a space of growth with compassion for yourself and how you would like to move forward.

Chapter 8

And the lesson is????

As I was about half way through writing this book, it occurred to me to

add this chapter. We hear all of the time, that there is a reason everything

happens, and I think for the most part I have always been able to look back

and understand and even appreciate why some things worked out they way

they did. A lot of times though, the reason things happen the way they do

is less than clear. I think we have a responsibility to look for that reason.

When I say look for that reason, I mean that sometimes, things just don't make sense, and we have an opportunity to look at hard situations and ask ourselves what we can stand to learn, even in the face of adversity and pain.

One night while writing this book, Jeff and I were out in the backyard of our home. We were discussing and trying to make sense of some really difficult conversations that were being had with his daughters' mother. Being a step parent is anything but easy, and while I happen to think I have the best step daughter in the world, it doesn't always mean it's easy to navigate the feelings that come with her not being mine biologically. The only reason I even bring biology up, is that it means there is a third party in our family more often than we'd like sometimes. Jeff has always put his daughter and I and our family first, and for that I have never doubted I am exactly where I needed to be, but that's not to say it hasn't been without heart ache and struggle on both sides. Jeff's daughter wasn't even two years old when I came into her life, and something we started saying the older she got, was that mommy grew her in her tummy and I grew her in my heart. She knows she has a mommy a daddy and a Lisa.

The amount of joy that I have experienced has been plentiful, and the lows have been there too. The particular night we were outside talking, the third party in our life had been making even the smallest details difficult. There was dentist appointment coming up that fell on our parenting day, which would mean Jeff would pick his daughter up at school around lunch and take her to the appointment. The third party didn't see the sense in taking her out of school for such an appointment and stated she would just keep her all day with her until the appointment.

While from a distance this might seem harmless, it was just another hurdle in the difficulties that we faced often. Jeff's ex wife struggled with the fact that he was awarded primary custody, and therefore the thought of Jeff showing up to an appointment with his daughter might make it look like his ex wife wasn't in control, and that was a reality she just couldn't bear to let anyone see.

While Jeff and I knew the reason for a lot of her decisions was to maintain a facade or narrative that she was in control, it didn't make our stress levels any less. I rarely had interaction with her aside from pick ups when I took Jeff's daughter back to her, but the emotional fall out of some pretty deceptive choices in an attempt to cut Jeff out of his daughters life, meant that even the slightest difficulty, came with a lot more than stress for Jeff. It seemed most days even things as simple as a dentist appointment, came with multiple messages and verbal judo until his ex felt like she was in control. It was a never ending negotiation, and when boundaries were set, she escalated.

It was a reminder of what might have been had he not had the courage to call this woman out and fight for his daughter. It was difficult for both of us, but for very different reasons. It was difficult for me to watch Jeff go through this on an almost daily basis some weeks, and it was difficult for Jeff to accept the reality of whom he had a child with.

On this particular night, we sat in the backyard after his daughter had gone to bed, and just tried to make sense of why even the smallest of tasks was a negotiation and a series of messages that rarely led anywhere productive. I asked him, "So, what's the lesson? I really don't understand what the lesson we are supposed to be learning form this is. It's senseless and constant and is hard on both of us."

Jeff looked at me with his gentle eyes and said, " I guess the first thing that comes to mind, is to trust your gut before you marry someone, it doesn't just get better."

Well, there's a lesson I too learned the hard way. I knew there was more to learn here, but for the life of me couldn't come up with anything, until I remembered a conversation I had with my mother a few weeks prior. I called her one night and was telling her about the third party's resistance to taking Jeff's daughter to school at all, not just the day of the dentist appointment. I couldn't understand why she wouldn't want her child to be around friends and start to get ready for kindergarten. On the surface I knew it was because she didn't choose the school, and when given an opportunity to have a say, refused, but deep down I just wanted to talk it out with my mom. I was concerned, because I thought that Jeff's daughter was going to suffer as a consequence of inconsistency, and we were noticing a few behaviors that we were trying to redirect.

I cried to my mom, and said,"I just don't know what to do and am so tired of feeling like I am one step behind. It feels like we are constantly on the lookout for behavior or statements or other things to redirect, to help make sure this doesn't effect her adversely as she grows up."

My mom said to me, "Lisa, stop trying to have all of the answers, you don't. When you can accept that you don't have all the answers you can be a little kinder to yourself, and actually step back and see the beautiful job you are doing with her."

That's when it occurred to me, that there is in fact a lesson here. I do believe that everything happens for a reason, but I also believe that sometimes it is our job to figure out what that reason or lesson is.

The lesson here is that I don't have all the answers and that's ok, but I do need to pay attention to how rigid and tense I get, so I can take care of myself and create an environment of compassion for myself and those around me. I can't imagine any of this has been easy on the third party either. I do have empathy for how much she clings to the need for control and can't imagine that is good space to be. My hope in my quietest moments is that we all three can look at this incredible little girl that we are lucky enough to have in our lives and find a space of compassion for each other. Until that day comes, I know what I can control is the space of compassion I create for myself and for my family. It really all goes back to my mantra I remind myself of daily, and that is, even in the toughest of situations, when you re being verbally attacked and insulted, you just don't treat people as bad as they are you treat them as good as you are.

In life we have a choice, get bitter or get better. While some days are harder than others, I have committed to getting better. There are just so many things and people in life that we can't control, and the only person we ever really have control over is ourselves and how we show up for ourselves on a daily basis. I can't even begin to image what our life would be like, if Jeff and I didn't make a choice each day to show up for our family first, and to lead with love. I feel grateful everyday of my life, that he and I choose each other and our family, and as a result have shared so many moments of laughter and love as a couple and as a family. His kindness and courage are inspiring to say the least. His ability to live, laugh and love after all he has been through in his life are truly a gift to those around him.

This is a man who served his country, and came home and now serves his fellow veterans in a cardiac Cath lab 5 days a week. He is in many ways my hero, and most nights when I think what in hell is the lesson, all I need to do is watch him, and my heart immediately is reminded, that the lesson is always love. The lesson when you don't know where to turn is always more love. Sometimes, it is more love for yourself an what you are going through, and other times it is more love for others around you.

It's imperative sometimes to look for creative ways to use that love and compassion. Sometimes you need to give a little more to someone else, and sometimes that love has to be given to yourself. What's the worst that can happen if you find out you aren't perfect? You accept that you're human and are allowed to have emotions that are hard and heavy. Acknowledge them, ask yourself why you're feeling that way, and then create a space of love and compassion so you can sort thought them.

Challenge yourself to give that gift to yourself daily, soften, take the tension out and let love and compassion for yourself and your struggle lead. Motivate yourself to do hard things and get through hard things, by motivating with love, not anger. Anger has a tendency to cloud your judgement whether you realize it or not, so feel it when you need to but don't stay stuck there, move through it to move forward.

Life and the people you encounter in it, both good and bad are the best kind of school you can attend. The price of admission is only that you commit to the idea that every conflict, every person, every good time and every bad one is all a lesson if you take the time to look. To allow yourself to blame people for something but then decide what you choose to do with it. The only other caveat is that you commit to showing up daily to this wild ride. Show up every day and challenge yourself to remember that you can only connect as far as you've connected to yourself, you can only trust as much as you trust yourself to be okay if things go wrong, and you can only give to others what you have first given to yourself.

Assignment #8

Grab your journal and make a list of people or situations that feel heavy and hard right now. Think about these situations and how you're approaching them, and then start to ask yourself, what is the lesson to learn here. What is repeating itself, what doesn't feel good, what do I think I need, what do I need to accept? When you ask yourself what do I need to accept about this situation or person, remember that acceptance doesn't mean you say their behavior is ok with you, it means you drop the need for a different outcome and work within the reality that is.

These questions if answered open and honestly will start to get you to a place of finding the lesson and taking charge. If you're having a hard time with this, maybe just being mindful of the situation and watching how you react to it in the coming weeks, will help you get to a place of seeing the lesson. Give yourself time and space to be mindful of your feelings and what is triggering you about the person and situation. The beauty in this assignment is that there are no right or wrong answers, but you do need to be honest about how you're feeling and what you can be accountable for in the situation.

Chapter 9

So, wait a minute, Who am I?

Hopefully by now you have a journal full of thoughts and feelings that you're getting excited about exploring and using to connect to yourself. These thoughts and feelings are not just lists, but they are the roadmap to carving out your self identity and cultivating a connection to your worth and yourself that you can be proud of. Don't just write things down and move on, revisit them to think about them and the impact they have on the direction of your life.

Thriving in life will look different for everyone. Our dreams, desires, and needs are all unique to us as individuals. The one constant that you must adopt in order to thrive, is the ability to push through fear. There will always be a reason not to try something and to stay stuck, but if you never find the strength to push, you will never find out what's on the other side. For some people, pushing through discomfort and fear might mean leaving a relationship they have been afraid to for fear of hurting the other person or what it will feel like to be single. For others it might be walking into a busy coffee shop and ordering their favorite drink while keeping their social anxiety in check. In each example, the strength to push through discomfort is what equates to thriving on your own terms. When you focus on your problems, you will most certainly find more problems, but when you focus on the possibilities, you will most definitely find more opportunity, the choice is yours.

Before you go any further, I have one more assignment in your journal that I'd like you to start to think about. The first thing I want you to do, is to block out all of the noise, perceptions and opinions that society and those around you have placed on you. When you can sit with yourself for a few moments in quiet and in a place of non judgement and acceptance, I'd like you to start to make a list of values that you believe in and can commit to. If you took the time to do this earlier in the book, that's great! If you didn't, that's ok, do it now. After you have done that, I want you to review that list and make sure after all of your journaling and discovery you still feel good about it.

A lot of times I think we think at this stage in our life that of course we know what our value system is, but I would challenge you to really think about whether or not you do. So what I'd like you to do now is grab your journal and write down a list of about 10 values that you feel like you can commit to and use as the foundation of your self identity and connection with yourself. If you're stuck on what a value is or what might feel good to you, then go ahead and search lists of values on the Internet, you'll be surprised at what you come up with and how many there are. After you've made your list of values I'd like you to sit back and reflect on those and first ask yourself how aligned am I with how I'm behaving and what this value system is. Do my actions get me closer to my value system or further away?

Then I'd like you to look at the list and prioritize them from most important being number one to least important being number ten. What is most important to you regarding who you are and how you navigate the world? Make that your number one. Allow yourself the space to think about the kinds of things that make you proud of yourself and that feel good to YOU, not anyone else.

Doing this exercise and being mindful of your value system in all that you do, is going to help keep you on the track of knowing who you are and exactly how you need to behave in each situation you encounter. When we are faced with a tough decision a lot of times people say I don't know what to do, I'm really bad at making decisions, and to that I say indecision is perfectionism in disguise. You don't have to be perfect to be worthy. You do however, need a foundation or a guide while you're getting used to this to know how to make tough decisions. The framework for making those tough decisions and feeling good about the choices you make is knowing who you are and what your value system is.

After you've done this, I just want you to page through the notes that you have in your journal so far. I'd like you to remember that forgiving yourself for past mistakes or struggles is imperative to moving forward from an empowered place. Remember, you don't ever start over you always start with experience, and sometimes that is the reassurance we need to remind ourselves that being human is okay.

After my divorce, it became crystal clear to me that on one hand I was finding my worth and figuring out who I was, but on the other hand so much of me had been changed from that experience. I missed the girl who was spontaneous, was fun loving, and trusting of all of those around me. I missed the girl who wasn't afraid to try new things, meet new people, and just basically throw caution to the wind. While I saw parts of her and knew she was in there somewhere I was having a really hard time after the divorce finding the girl I once was, and found myself often times grieving and confused about why I couldn't find her. When I wasn't confused or grieving the anger would creep in at myself and my ex-husband for changing a part of me that I had grown to love so much.

Then one day, after over thinking over analyzing and trying to figure out who I was and where I was going, it hit me. I was never going to find the girl I was before I married him, she didn't exist anymore, she was better, she was different, and that was OK! While I saw parts of her from time to time I think there was a part of me looking to go back to who I was before I married him to erase that time in my life that I wasn't proud of. When I realized what I was doing and why I was doing it I was able to create a space in my life where I fell in love with the unknown and was able to ask myself, who am I now? That was a defining moment for me in my healing process and connecting to my worth.

When I was able to start asking myself who am I now, I was able to take all of the experience from that marriage the heart ache ,the hard times and the good ones and start to create a self identity that I felt proud of, and that was a product of the experience. When I created a space to fall in love a bit with the unknown, I also found snippets of the girl I was before I married him. I found myself giving myself permission to find the best parts of her, and create different parts of me moving forward that wouldn't repeat the same patterns. When I gave myself permission to create that identity, to commit to a value system that only I got to choose, that's when I started to feel proud of who I was.

That was an all encompassing journey for me, because it meant I also had to accept the fact that the coping skills I picked up in childhood, my patterns of people pleasing and wanting to be chosen, weren't working for me as an adult. I had to stop thinking that something was wrong with me, and allow myself the space to acknowledge what wasn't working, in order to create the space to choose myself. When I was able to recognize that the coping skills I picked up in childhood weren't working for me as an adult, I learned how to choose me without anyone choosing me first. I started to seek out opportunities to validate myself, and let the adult version of me that I had created take control rather than my inner child who stopped at nothing to feel valid and find external validation. I learned how to give validation to myself first. I learned that if I didn't learn to fill myself up first, I had nothing but resentment, anger, and desperation to give to others. Most importantly, I learned that validating my adult self, meant first validating and loving the inner child when she showed up as well.

After you're done reviewing the notes that you have carved out in your journal I'd like you to just sit and think about all that you have written and discovered through this process. Sitting with them for a moment and being proud of yourself for the vulnerability and work that you've put in this far is an important step to getting ready to bring it all together. I want you to get excited about the opportunity to figure out what from the past you're carrying with you that's not working, and think about what you'd like to keep, and where you'd like to go next.

Grab your journal, and carve out some quiet time where you get to sit alone with you and your story. I don't want you to overthink too much I just want you to start to practice trusting yourself and your intuition and I want you to just start writing.

I'd like you to start at the beginning and just start writing your story down. Start from the beginning, or as far back as you can remember and use this as an exercise to not only appreciate and have compassion for where you've been, but understand how it's affecting you in your present day life. Pushing your story down and not acknowledging how it may have affected how you operate in present day doesn't help you, but just really only throws gas on the fire. As the title of the book states it's going to be great, I want you to know that whatever you choose and whoever you choose to be it is going to be great, but first you have to look at where you've been to really appreciate and empower yourself to know where you're going.

I want you to acknowledge your past and get really honest with yourself about where you've been, choices you've made, the stories and narratives you're hiding behind, what you're afraid of, what's keeping you stuck, and where you want to go. If you can start today by putting the work in to connecting with *your* worth and being proud of who you are, you will start to navigate the world in a way that feels right to you.

Starting the process of creating who you are and not being victim to patterns of your past, means today you commit to choosing alignment over validation from others, peace over addictive chaos and being misunderstood to false acceptance.

If you're nearing the end of the book, and thinking to yourself I'm still struggling with connecting to my self-worth, I really want you to sit with that for a moment. I'd like it to challenge you to remember that if you're still struggling to see that it's something you cultivate and create by your internal dialogue being a positive one, by the choices you make that are becoming of your worth, then it's safe to say it was something you were taught that you chase outside of yourself instead of within. I also want you to remember that this is a relationship you cultivate and show up to daily, rarely is it something that clicks for people after reading one book or overnight but rather is the result of lots of little moments and opportunities to validate yourself and connect to your worth. It's these thoughts and actions that build into a bigger stronger healthier relationship with yourself and your self-worth. Consistency and accountability are the name of the game, give yourself some patience and time as you figure it out.

My wish for you, is that by acknowledging what doesn't feel good and what isn't quite working for you, that you learn that it is okay to start by letting go of other people's opinion about YOUR life. I hope you come to realize that there is no right or wrong way to live a life that feels good to you, but rather learn to accept we all have different definitions of thriving and living. Because of these differences, some people will judge you or call you difficult or different, let them, it's ok. If you stumble and allow other people and their opinions to alter your course, you end up living someone else's life.

I also wish that you don't allow other's fear of vulnerability and passion for life, hinder yours. I want you to be open to this world and the people in it. Don't hold back or filter yourself for fear of what others may think, be committed to being about what you think.

I hope you learn to fall in love with the unknown and understand that your path in this life will not be a perfect one, but will be a real one that is yours to celebrate and embrace. All of it.

My final and maybe most important wish for you, is that you learn to let go of things and people that don't love you back and the stories you tell yourself that make that okay. I hope that you learn to let go of the hurt, the shame, and the feeling that you aren't worthy of real love and that you need to settle for less than you deserve. You don't. You wake up each and every day with an opportunity to not be bound to your past, no matter how old you are. It is never too late to love yourself, create new patterns moving forward, and give yourself the same love you so fiercely give to others.

The truth is, it is going to be great and you are going to be just fine, as long you start today, taking charge of your life and living one that is authentic on the inside and the outside. There is no age limit to life's ups and downs, and remember that right now is right on time. Push through fear, welcome mistakes, laugh at the ridiculousness that life sometimes brings our way, and settle in to the adventure of navigating it and welcoming the unknown. Start today and make a choice to thrive not just survive, YOU ARE WORTH IT!!